DIVING AND SNORKELING GUIDE TO

Northern California and the Monterey Peninsula Second Edition

Steve Rosenberg

Pisces Books

Acknowledgments

Thank you to my wife, Kathleen, Nancy Guarascio, Al Huelga, Conrad Lauer, Bob McCurdy, and Harry White for their assistance and encouragement in putting this book together.

All photographs are by the author

Copyright © 1992 by Lonely Planet Publications
Head Office: PO Box 617, Hawthorn, Vic 3122, Australia
Branches: 150 Linden St, Oakland, CA 94607, USA
10a Spring Place, London NW5 3BH, UK
71 bis rue du Cardinal Lemoine, 75005 Paris, France

Library of Congress Cataloging-in-Publication Data
Rosenberg, Steve, 1948–
Diving and snorkeling guide to northern California and the Monterey Peninsula/Steve Rosenberg.—2nd ed.
p. cm.
Includes index.
ISBN 1-55992-052-1
1. Scuba diving—California, Northern—Guide-books.
2. Skin diving—California, Northern—Guide-books.
3. California, Northern—Description and travel—Guide-books. I. Title. II. Title: Northern California and the Monterey Peninsula.
GV840.S78R64 1992
797.2′3′09794—dc20 91-23031
CIP

> **Publisher's Note:** At the time of publication of this book, all the information was determined to be as accurate as possible. However, when you use this guide, new construction may have changed land reference points, weather may have altered reef configurations, and some businesses may no longer be functioning. Your assistance in keeping future editions up-to-date will be greatly appreciated.
>
> Also, please pay particular attention to the diver rating system in this book. Know your limits!

Printed in Hong Kong

Contents

How to Use This Guide

This guide will be a useful tool for divers who are either residents of California or visitors, regardless of their level of skill. The book covers two major areas—the Monterey Peninsula and the California North Coast—and provides detailed information about the more popular dive sites.

The information given for each dive site will enable the reader to dive safely and to get the maximum enjoyment from each dive. Each dive site description includes the location and/or directions to the site, dive entry and exit points, range of depths, on-site facilities, and a brief description of the underwater topography and marine life. This information should help you select those dive sites most appropriate to your level of skill and personal interests.

Diving in Northern and Central California is quite different from warm-water diving. Cold water temperatures require that you wear either a quarter-inch wetsuit or a drysuit. The emphasis on beach diving coupled with the conditions, which can be rough at some sites, requires training that isn't necessary in other dive areas. If you're a novice diver or if you're new to California, it's a good idea to buddy up with an experienced local diver. Consult the local dive stores; they can give you up-to-date information on charter boats and current weather conditions.

If you choose to take your first dive without the benefit of a local diver's experience, don't overestimate your ability; choose a site that is well-protected from the open ocean. Do not attempt to beach dive in an area where there is heavy surf or strong currents, and keep in mind that tides and wave action can drastically change the conditions at any particular site very quickly. This is especially true on the North Coast, as many of the sites there are exposed to the prevailing winds and swells that roll in from the northwest. Even experienced divers contact a local dive store for information on diving conditions before setting out for a dive site, and will cancel their plans to dive on a moment's notice if the conditions aren't right for a safe, enjoyable excursion.

The octopus is usually a nocturnal predator, but in Monterey Bay the shy animals are often seen foraging during the day. ➤

The Rating System for Divers and Dives

It is important to be conservative when reviewing the minimum level of expertise recommended for the dives in this guide. Keep in mind the adage that there are old divers and bold divers, but few old, bold divers. We consider a *novice diver* to be someone in decent physical condition who has recently completed a basic diving certification course, or is a certified diver who has not been diving recently, or who has no experience in similar waters. We consider an *intermediate diver* to be a certified diver in excellent physical condition who has been diving actively for at least a year following certification in a basic diving course, and who has been diving recently in similar waters. We consider an *advanced diver* to be someone who has completed an advanced certification diving course, or who has the equivalent experience, has been diving recently in similar waters, has been diving frequently for at least two years, and is in excellent physical condition.

Diving in Northern and Central California requires the use of a wetsuit or drysuit because of the cold water temperatures.

You will have to decide for yourself if you're capable of making a particular dive, depending on your level of training, experience, and physical condition, as well as water conditions at the site. Remember that water conditions can change at any time, even during a dive.

The recommended diving locations included in this guide have been divided into two sections, the Monterey Peninsula and the North Coast. The section on Monterey includes some sites suitable for novice divers to try on their own, and some which should be attempted only by advanced divers.

The section on the North Coast has some sites which can be dived by novices, but even on these dives, it is strongly recommended that novices be accompanied by an advanced diver or instructor. Most of the North Coast areas are rated for intermediate or advanced divers, and these ratings are based on favorable water conditions. When the ocean is rough, there are very few North Coast locations which can be dived at all.

The rating of a site is always based on ideal water conditions. Always check with a local dive store to get an update on weather and water conditions which might affect the ratings listed.

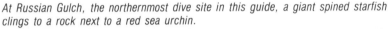

At Russian Gulch, the northernmost dive site in this guide, a giant spined starfish clings to a rock next to a red sea urchin.

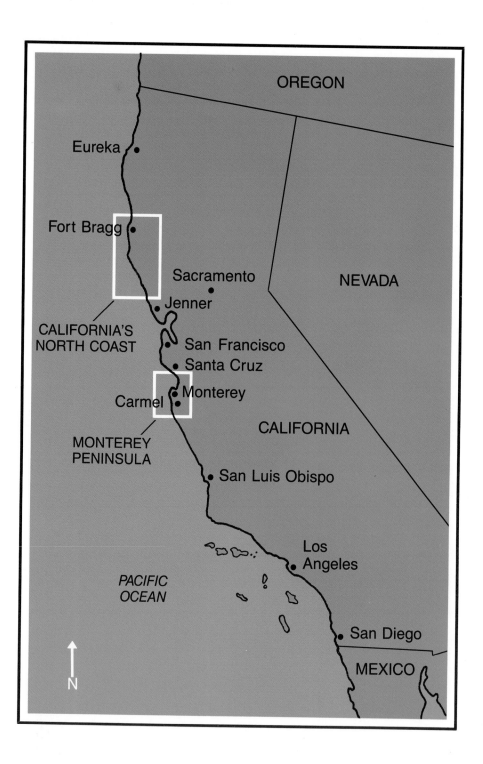

OREGON

Eureka

Fort Bragg

Sacramento

NEVADA

Jenner

CALIFORNIA'S
NORTH COAST

San Francisco

Santa Cruz

Monterey

Carmel

MONTEREY
PENINSULA

CALIFORNIA

San Luis Obispo

PACIFIC
OCEAN

Los
Angeles

San Diego

N

MEXICO

Overview of Central and Northern California

The coast of central and northern California is best known for its rugged shoreline. Rocky headlands and promontories rise vertically, alternating with stretches of recessed shoreline bordered with sand and gravel beaches. The rugged shoreline is quite straight, broken only by the Monterey and San Francisco bays. Deep underwater canyons reach into Monterey Bay and neighboring Carmel Bay. North of San Francisco, there are a number of smaller bays following the San Andreas fault line, which extend into the sea just to the south of Cape Mendocino. Along the central and northern coast, high cliffs and elevated terraces rise from the sea.

To understand why California's marine life is so diverse, it helps to have a general understanding of the forces that shaped the coastline and created this incredibly rich environment.

During the Pleistocene Age, which occurred about 20,000 years ago, vast portions of North America were covered by immense sheets of ice. The formation of these ice sheets lowered the sea level by more than 400 feet (120 meters), thus exposing previously submerged coastal areas. South of the ice sheet, new coastal plains emerged and, in California, extended as much as 60 miles (97 kilometers) beyond today's shoreline. Rivers formed and cut channels through the plains, creating deltas and estuaries along the new coast. Their beds, cut into the surround rock, are now submarine canyons.

When the ice melted about 12,000 years ago, the sea level rose again, flooding low valleys and river mouths. Water flooding seaward from the melting ice swelled the rivers, which produced some of California's most striking coastal cliffs and wide beaches. The rivers gradually eroded the soft rock formations—sandstone, clay and shale—while the harder rock developed into headlands. The result was the formation of massive cliffs jutting into the water that alternate with recessed stretches of sandy beach, giving the coast a scalloped appearance.

From shore, the Continental Shelf gradually slopes down to approximately 600 feet (185 meters) before plunging sharply into the depths of the

Some of the best diving in California is to be had in the area around the Monterey Peninsula and the coastal waters from Jenner to Fort Bragg. Little diving is done in the San Francisco area because of heavy surge, poor visibility, and the presence of great white sharks in the Farallon Island vicinity. Great whites frequent this "triangle" because of the presence of seals and other marine animals on which these sharks feed. Diving in Southern California and the Channel Islands is covered in separate diving guides.

Pacific Ocean. In the coastal areas above the Shelf marine life feasts on a plentiful supply of nutrients, fostering a riotous profusion of both vertebrate and invertebrate life.

When the Spanish explorer Balboa first laid eyes on the vast sea that borders California he called it the "Pacific," or peaceful, ocean. That is an apt description for the waters off Panama, where Balboa first saw the ocean, but hardly accurate for the area off Central and Northern California.

Diving along the northern California coast is often done from shore. Many divers use inflatable boats, dive boards and surf mats to help them get from the beach to the best dive spots.

The plants and animals that live along the California coast have had to adapt to the rigors of the strong currents, heavy waves and strong tides that buffet the coastal zone. They are also challenged by variable levels of light, water temperature, oxygen levels, and salt content.

Currents. The southward-flowing California Current parallels the California coast until it reaches the equator, where it heads west. The Current is part of the current system of the Pacific Ocean. Spawned by winds and the rotation of the earth, warm equatorial waters flow west to Asia, where they head north in the vast Kuroshio Current. The Kuroshio

Current passes Japan and turns east, heading for North America. Along the way, it picks up cooler water drawn down from the Arctic and eventually turns south, becoming the California Current. As it sweeps along the coast, the Current carries with it billions of microscopic plankton and other marine plants and animals that feed the coastal marine life.

The currents and the strong winds of the Pacific team up to generate some of the most powerful waves in the Northern Hemisphere. The waves and currents gnaw at the shoreline, continuously resculpting the beaches and wearing down the rocky headlands. The currents and waves help bring nutrients into shallow areas near shore, as do upwelling currents, which pulls cold, rich water up from the depths to help nourish life in the coastal zone.

The effect of tides on the formation of the California coast is second only to the powerful waves. In some places, tides play a critical role in transporting sediment. Each day along the Pacific Coast, there are usually

California sea lions are only one of the many marine mammals found in the Monterey area. Divers can often encounter these playful animals in many of the sites covered in this book.

two high tides and two low tides, all of unequal height. The movement of tidal waters near the shore causes tidal currents. As the tide rises, the waters flow toward shore causing a flood tide. During ebb tide, the water moves out, exposing low-lying coastal areas.

Formation of Rocky Areas. Rocky areas are present where there are hard rock outcroppings along the coast and in coastal waters where there is sufficient water movement to prevent the rock from being buried by soft sediment. Rocky areas also form where the rock face is too steep to allow sediment to collect. Of course, other factors also shape rock formation: direction and size of waves, direction and speed of offshore currents, frequency of storms, the nature and rate of erosion, the steepness of the slope where sea meets land, and the recent geological history of the region. All of these factors have created an unique and breathtaking topography—both on land and underwater.

Sea otters are gregarious and cuddly looking habitues of the central California coast, where they hunt shellfish and crabs in the shallow waters of coves and inlets.

Diving in Central and Northern California

Majestic rock formations, marine mammals, vast underwater kelp forests, and an array of colorful invertebrates and other marine animals await you in the waters along the central and northern California coast.

Water Temperature. The water temperature in this region is affected by a number of factors, including depth and currents. Surface temperatures range from 50–56 degrees Fahrenheit (10–16 degrees Celsius), depending on the location. The temperatures stay constant down to depths of 30–40 feet (10–12 meters). Nevertheless, you will often encounter significantly colder temperatures in deeper water—as low as 45 degrees Fahrenheit (7 degrees Celsius)—due to thermoclines or deep water upwellings. Recently, warm currents from the south, called El Ninos, have warmed the surface temperatures by as much as 15 degrees Fahrenheit for short periods of time. This has attracted some species of marine life that are usually only found in waters far to the south. Most local divers wear a minimum quarter-inch wet suit to protect themselves against the cold. Dry suits, which help keep divers warm for long periods of time, have become popular among the local sport divers.

Dive Seasons. Diving is enjoyed throughout the year in the Monterey area. The fall and winter months, when plankton growth is the lowest, usually provide the best visibility. Though the climate is moderate for most of the year, there is no way of forecasting the dive conditions on any given day. The average visibility in Monterey Bay is 20–40 feet (6–12 meters), with visibility sometimes exceeding 60 feet (18 meters) along the outer reefs and in the Point Lobos State Reserve, located on the southern edge of Carmel Bay.

Along the north coast, the dive season is determined not so much by the water conditions, though water temperature and visibility do have an effect, but by the fishing seasons. Abalone diving and spearfishing are the two most popular activities in this region. The California Department of Fish and Game restricts abalone diving north of Yankee Point to April through June and August through November. Most of the organized spearfishing expeditions occur during the spring and summer months.

Kelp Diving. Kelp forests, a rich habitat for marine life, are popular among experienced divers. Novice divers, or divers who have never had the pleasure of diving in California's kelp beds, may at first be a bit nervous, but once you learn the basics of kelp diving, you'll quickly find that there's little to fear. In fact, kelp can be an aid to divers. These long strands of seaweed can show you which way the current is flowing. In areas where there is a lot of boat traffic, kelp can indicate safe areas in which to surface. Kelp beds are also a good area to tie off small boats, rafts, and dive floats. But perhaps the best incentive to try kelp diving is the spectacular selection of marine life which lives in these areas.

Mendocino County is among the most breathtakingly scenic places in North America; much of the coastline consists of steep cliffs that plunge almost vertically to rocky shores below.

Of course, kelp can be hazardous if you get caught in it and panic. Be particularly aware of kelp at the surface where it can become so thick that you can't swim through it. Always ascend with a reserve of air so that you can descend and, if necessary, find a clear opening through which to surface.

All abalone diving north of Yankee Point must be done while free diving. Consequently, diving in kelp presents further difficulties. Try to stay away from areas where kelp is extremely thick and always be aware of surface kelp while ascending. And *never* try to fight through a layer of kelp to get to the surface.

Sculpins, like this tiny one hiding in an empty shell in Monterey Bay, are found in depths from the intertidal down to 70 feet.

Beach Diving. Most of the diving in northern and central California is beach diving, so you should be aware of the accepted safety techniques for entering and exiting the water. Although there are some minor differences in the skills taught in certification courses, it is generally held that, except on extremely calm days, divers should be wearing fins, have their regulators in their mouths, and back into the surf. In heavy surf, exit the water by crawling on all fours through the surf line, with your regulator in your mouth. It is also recommended that you reserve between 500 and 1000 psi for your exit, and select an alternate exit in case the surf becomes dangerously rough at your preferred exit point during the course of the dive.

Different rules apply on the north coast where there are few sandy beaches. Be aware of rip currents and coastal currents, and be prepared to abort the dive when the conditions are hazardous. If you are a novice diver or are not familiar with the area, it is better to buddy up with an experienced diver who is familiar with the sites you want to dive.

Boat Diving. In Monterey there are several dive boats now operating, together with a veritable fleet of inflatables. The dive charters are listed in the Appendix.

Because of their stability, fairly low cost, low maintenance, maneuverability, and versatility as a dive platform, inflatables have become very popular.

Inflatables have become popular, and with good reason. They are stable, relatively inexpensive, require little maintenance, are easy to maneuver, and double as a dive platform. But the number of boat ramps available on the Monterey Peninsula is limited. There are two double ramps inside the Monterey Breakwater, a facility at Stillwater Cove (Pebble Beach), and a small ramp at Point Lobos, which can only be used for diving inside the reserve. On the north coast there are a number of launch sites which will accommodate small inflatables, and a few facilities which permit medium and large inflatables and aluminum boats to be launched.

A few safety rules about diving from inflatables: Many divers anchor their boat, leaving the vessel unattended. Be sure to check the anchor at the beginning of the dive to make sure that it is firmly set on the bottom. It could be quite an inconvenience if you were to surface and find no boat in sight. Also, because ocean swells can quickly increase in size, let out at least 50 percent more anchor line than the depth where you are anchored. For example, if the water is 50 feet (15 meters) deep, let out at least 75 feet (23 meters) of rope. It is also a good idea to begin the dive by swimming up current. And, you should come up with at least 500 psi so that you can locate the boat and swim back to it underwater if the kelp is thick at the surface.

2

Diving on the Monterey Peninsula

The Monterey Peninsula, from Del Monte Beach in Monterey Bay to the Point Lobos State Reserve at the southern end of Carmel Bay, is by far the most popular dive area in central and northern California. If you've never dived in Monterey's magnificent kelp forests or explored its underwater canyons, it's understandable that you'd wonder why so many divers enthusiastically jump into water that's 50 degrees Fahrenheit (10 degrees Celsius). Indeed, tourists strolling along Monterey's secluded beaches or dining at any number of romantic restaurants in Carmel watch these divers with fascination. But, until they take the plunge, they'll never know what beauty awaits them in the depths along the peninsula.

The beauty and excitement of diving this area far outweigh the hassle of dealing with erratic surf, the cold water temperatures, and the inconvenience of a full wet suit or dry suit. The waters may be chilly compared to warmer climes, but there are sights that warm-water enthusiasts will never witness: playful sea lions and otters, majestic birds swooping from the sky, incredible kelp forests, and colorful reefs are just a few of the attractions.

Here, most diving is done from the shore. Beach diving, where some amount of surf is the rule, requires special skills. If you're visiting Monterey for the first time, limit your initial dives to those areas where the entries and exits are well protected. It is always a good idea to talk with local divers and, if possible, find a dive buddy who is familiar with the area.

Monterey Peninsula offers so many tourist attractions that traffic is heavy. As a result, many local municipalities have passed ordinances restricting parking, gearing up, and beach-related activities. Be aware that some of the dive locations, including parts of Pacific Grove, Hopkins Reef, and Point Lobos, are marine reserves where all plants and animals are protected. The local dive stores will be able to brief you on fish and game laws, as well as weather, surf, and visibility.

Diving around the Monterey Peninsula is generally divided into two geographic regions: Monterey Bay and Carmel Bay.

The strawberry anemone is common on rocky reefs in areas where there is a lot of water movement. They come in a variety of pastel colors including pink, orange, and lavender. ➤

Divers at Hopkins Reef get a terrific oceanside view of Monterey's famed Cannery Row. The Monterey Aquarium, which is worth a visit, is located at the end of Cannery Row.

Monterey Bay. Dive sites inside the bay are generally protected from the prevailing northwest swells. With the exception of Outer Chase Reef at the southern tip of the bay and outer Hopkins Reef, most of the dive locations are fairly shallow, with depths ranging from 20–70 feet (6–21 meters). The visibility rarely exceeds 30 feet, and the best visibility occurs during the fall and early winter, when there's the least amount of plankton. Water temperatures range from 51 to 56 degrees Fahrenheit (11 to 13 degrees Celsius).

Carmel Bay. By contrast, water temperatures in Carmel Bay range from 49 to 52 degrees Fahrenheit (9 to 12 degrees Celsius) at the surface, and can drop as low as 46 degrees Fahrenheit (8 degrees Celsius) at lower depths. If you can withstand the cold, you're in for a spectacular dive.

In Carmel Bay, the submarine canyon rises up to within 200 yards (185 meters) of the shore at the north end of Monastery Beach. The canyon drops off sharply at that point, falling to well over 1,000 feet (307 meters) just one mile north of Point Lobos. Then, continuing to the northwest, the canyon plummets to over 7,000 feet (2.2 kilometers) just six miles away,

Many of Monterey's kelp beds are close to shore with access from shore. A couple prepares to dive from shore, attired in drysuits to keep them comfortably warm in Monterey's chilly waters.

where it meets the Monterey Bay submarine canyon. During the spring and summer months, northwesterly winds drive the surface waters out to sea, allowing waters rich in nutrients to rise from the depths of the trench. As a result, these waters support an impressive community of plants and animals.

The California Sea Otter. This creature is one of the most delightful and fascinating attractions of the Monterey Peninsula. Smaller than most other mammals that inhabit these waters, the otters measure four-and-one-half feet in length and weigh in at 60 pounds (27 kilograms) (females weigh approximately 40 pounds, or 18 kilograms). Unlike sea lions and harbor seals, otters do not have an insulating layer of fat. But their rapid metabolism and a layer of air bubbles trapped in their fur keep them warm. To maintain a high metabolic rate, otters must eat approximately 25 percent of their body weight every day. Their diet consists of over 40 kinds of invertebrates, including snails, starfish, sea urchins, clams, crab, abalone, and squid.

Monterey Bay

The Monterey area is a major tourist attraction, with an incredible array of excellent restaurants and quaint shops. The Monterey captured in John Steinbeck's "Cannery Row" is very much in evidence. It's almost as though the mountains that crowd the narrow shoulder of the peninsula have kept the area's picturesque past from disappearing. Much of the charm of Cannery Row has been preserved. Some new developments, such as the fabulous Monterey Bay Aquarium, have been built within the walls of the old cannery buildings.

The charm of this area doesn't end at the water's edge. Sea otters, once hunted almost to extinction, at least along the California coast, have staged a comeback and are now seen throughout the kelp beds along the shoreline of Monterey Bay. Sea lions, seals, brown pelicans, and other diving birds are very visible on the surface, providing entertainment for tourists and divers alike. Although the sardines that spawned Cannery Row are no longer present in great numbers, the diversity and abundance of marine life that remains in the area is unsurpassed anywhere.

California kelp beds provide a home to many types of interesting marine animals .

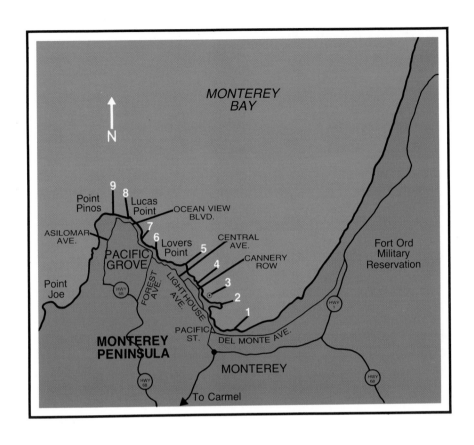

DIVE SITE RATINGS

	Novice	Intermediate	Advanced
1 Del Monte Beach		×	×
2 The Breakwater	×	×	×
3 Metridium Field		×	×
4 McAbee Beach	×	×	×
5 Hopkins Reef	×	×	×
6 Lover's Point Cove	×	×	×
7 Otter Cove		×	×
8 Coral Street Beach	×	×	×
9 Chase Reef		×	×

Typical depth range	:	30–60 feet (10–18 meters)
Typical water conditions	:	Moderate to heavy surf and surge, often limited visibility
Expertise required	:	Intermediate
Access	:	Beach

Del Monte Beach is the largest stretch of beach inside Monterey Bay. Here, most of the bottom is sandy and shallow, less than 40 feet (12 meters) deep for a good distance from shore. Approximately 100 yards (97 meters) from the beach are a series of low shale ledges, or shoals, running parallel to shore. Here you'll find a variety of marine life, including flounders, octopuses, blennies, sponges, anemones, and an occasional strand of kelp. Divers also report seeing many types of rays and skates parked on the ocean bottom. This area is often referred to as "Tanker Reef."

If wreck diving is your pleasure, you'll find several sunken barges in 40–50 feet (12–15 meters) of water not far from the Monterey Beach Hotel, just off Highway 1. Closer to shore, in less than 20 feet (6 meters) of water, fields of purple sand dollars pop out of the sand. Though inhabited by

Octopuses of all sizes are common sights on night dives inside of Monterey Bay. Although shy, they can sometimes be cornered for an intimate portrait.

A diver confronts a large, slow moving electric ray on the sand flats near Tanker Reef.

several varieties of fish and plants, this area often experiences heavy surge and low visibility. For this reason, the area does not attract a large number of divers except during halibut season (June through September).

One of the most popular places to hunt halibut along Del Monte Beach is a spot called "The Laundromat," named after the laundromat at the intersection of Park and Del Monte Avenues in Monterey—the closest access to the area. About 200 yards (185 meters) south of the end of Park Avenue are the remains of an old pier, which runs perpendicular to the shoals and beach. Halibut follow this artificial reef into the shallow waters, feeding on crustaceans in the sand.

Halibut have flat, elongated bodies and are usually found lying partially buried in the sand or mud. Halibut are very timid, and the appearance of a diver usually causes the fish to dart off suddenly, creating a virtual sand storm. But they usually return to the same spot, or swim only a short distance before settling back into the sand.

Typical depth range	:	20–60 feet (6–18 meters)
Typical water conditions	:	Calm, light surge
Expertise required	:	Novice
Access	:	Beach and boat ramps

The Breakwater is an excellent introduction to the variety of underwater sites you'll find in Monterey. Divers at all levels will find something of interest.

On the northwest side of the Monterey harbor is a manmade rock jetty which extends 200 yards (185 meters) into the bay from the end of the Coast Guard pier. This area is commonly referred to as the Breakwater. At the intersection of Cannery Row and Foam Street is a parking lot, restroom facilities and a double boat ramp. Another boat ramp is located next to the Harbor Master's office between piers one and two. You can access the narrow, rocky beach from stairs located on the outside of the Breakwater, and from a small park at the foot of Reeside Avenue, one block away. This is one of the safest entry points in Monterey and, therefore, is used frequently by diving instructors. The surf here is usually calm, allowing for easy entries and exits.

California sea lions can be found in large numbers sunning themselves on the rock jetty at the end of the Monterey Breakwater during most of the year.

A gopher rockfish pauses just inches away from the tentacles of a group of strawberry anemones and a larger solitary rose anemone.

On the ocean side, a kelp bed grows along the entire length of the breakwater. This is a good opportunity to get a feel for kelp diving without having to worry about rough surf or strong surge. The rock jetty slopes to a sandy bottom that's 50–60 feet (15–18 meters) deep, home to a splendid array of filter feeders, including tube anemones and sea pens. Playful sea lions, sea otters, diving birds, octopuses and monkeyface eels also inhabit the area. Because of the excellent diversity of marine invertebrates at the Breakwater, the area has become popular with underwater photographers, even though the visibility is usually not as good as in other parts of the Monterey Peninsula. The easy access and rock jetty provide good reference points underwater, making it an excellent site for night dives.

You'll find the best diving outside the rock jetty. Enter the water from the sand beach at the bottom of the stairs and swim to the point where the jetty bends slightly to the right before descending. If you swim all the way to the end of the jetty, you'll find as many as 40 young sea lions waiting for a playmate!

Typical depth range	:	50–70 feet (15–21 meters)
Typical water conditions	:	Light surge
Expertise required	:	Intermediate, with open water experience
Access	:	Boat

The Metridium Field lies in about 50–70 feet (15–21 meters) of water. It got its name from the hundreds of rocky outcroppings covered with billowy white metridium anemones, whose stalks extend up to two feet in length. It is located about 200 yards off shore at the intersection of a line drawn from the tip of the Breakwater to Cabrillo Point (Hopkins marine station) and a line drawn as an extension of Reeside Avenue.

Small octopuses and crabs forage among the tube anemones and sea pens that dot the sandy bottom. Divers here frequently see bat rays, juvenile wolf eels, ocean sunfish, and an occasional bull sea lion cruising the outcroppings. When visibility is good, it is possible to hover 20–30 feet (6–9 meters) from the bottom and literally scan acres of white anemones. Most of the time, though, visibility rarely exceeds 15–25 feet (5–8 meters) because of the concentration of plankton. On sunny days when the visibility is good, the Metridium Field is an excellent place for wide-angle photography.

You can swim to the area, but it's a fairly long journey. It's safer to dive from an inflatable or other boat. Anchor at the location given above and follow the anchor line to the bottom—approximately 60 feet (18 meters) down. Swim toward Cabrillo Point and slightly northwest to find the greatest concentration of outcroppings with anemones. Always check your anchor at the beginning of the dive to make sure it is securely set. It is also important to leave sufficient "scope" or slack in the anchor line to prevent sudden swells from yanking the anchor off the bottom.

Stalks of metridium anemones can be up to two-feet long, and are topped with large, fluffy plumes that help filter plankton from the surrounding water.

Typical depth range	:	25–35 feet (8–11 meters)
Typical water conditions	:	Light surf, surge
Expertise required	:	Novice
Access	:	Beach

This is another popular spot for scuba instructors. A thick kelp forest extends about 200 yards (185 meters) offshore. A jumbled rocky reef is inhabited by a multitude of marine denizens, including sea hares, crabs, chitons, anemones, and rockfish. Old decaying pipelines used by the caneries that once thrived along Cannery Row criss-cross the area. These pipelines now serve as an artificial reef, attracting rockfish and a myriad of invertebrates.

Divers must gear up in the parking lot a block away from Cannery Row and walk to the beach. The multilevel parking lot is a fee lot and has no restroom facilities. Most of the parking is taken up by visitors to Monterey's new aquarium, so arrive early in the day to make sure you get a parking spot. Be aware of restrictions on the loading and unloading of dive gear, which are clearly posted along Cannery Row.

Sea otters, the smallest of California's marine mammals, are commonly seen by divers in the kelp beds off the central part of the state.

Harbor seals play in the shallows of McAbee Beach and often follow divers around during a dive.

The entrance to the beach is located at the intersection of Cannery Row and Hoffman Street next to the Casa Maria restaurant. Swim straight out for at least 75 yards (70 meters) before descending in 25 feet (8 meters) of water. The bottom, which consists of a combination of rock shelves and sandy patches, slopes gently to a maximum depth of 35 feet (11 meters) at the outer edge of the kelp bed.

Typical depth range	:	30–60 feet (10–18 meters)
Typical water conditions	:	Light to moderate surge
Expertise required	:	Novice to intermediate in the shallow areas
Access	:	Boat, dive board

Hopkins Reef, located between the Monterey Aquarium and Point Cabrillo, is a protected marine reserve under study by marine biologists from Stanford University's Hopkins Marine Station. Divers should be extremely

Sea Hares are often found in the sandy channels between the rocky outcropping of Hopkins Reef.

careful not to disturb any of the research projects in progress. The reef is accessible by boat or dive board only, and the ban against spearfishing is strictly enforced.

The shallow areas (20–45 feet, or 6–14 meters) are marked by a thick kelp bed. Sea otters are frequently seen here rafting on the surface or foraging for food. The bottom is made up of large granite formations with patches of sand between them. As you work your way toward the outer edge of the kelp, the bottom drops away in terraces to fairly deep water.

Kelp clings to the rocks, as do nudibranchs, sea hares, sea stars, anemones, and crabs. The reef is also home to a variety of rockfish.

Dive boats should anchor outside the research area, which is clearly marked with buoys, to avoid doing any damage to the bottom.

Wolf eels are often seen on the deep terraces below 70 feet on the outside of Hopkins Reef.

Typical depth range	:	20–40 feet (6–12 meters)
Typical water conditions	:	Light surf on the east side of the point, light to moderate surf and surge on the ocean side
Expertise required	:	East side, novice; Ocean side, novice to intermediate
Access	:	Beach, boat

Located on Ocean View Boulevard at the end of 17th Street, Lover's Point is a scenic tourist attraction in Pacific Grove. In addition to sightseers, the area is popular among dive instructors and photographers. You can access the beach at points on the inside of the cove (east side) and from the ocean side. Access on the cove side is well protected from heavy surf by a short breakwater and the point itself. In addition, the cove has a gently sloping sandy beach. The small area of sandy beach on the east side of the point is used by a wide variety of groups competing for the limited space. These users include swimmers, sunbathers, snorkelers, surfers, and families with little children. Therefore, from April through September, Friday through Monday, scuba access to the water over the east cove beach is limited to mornings before 11:30. No scuba gear can be left on the beach area.

The east side of Lover's Point provides a sheltered entry point for divers. The best diving is around the point, to the left of the beach as you swim out.

Victor Hugo's Quasimodo has nothing on the monkeyface eels—actually a type of fish— which are common around Lover's Point.

Entry from the west side of the point can be hazardous when the waves are rough. Restroom facilities are available in the park area overlooking the ocean. There is limited parking along Ocean View Boulevard and the two-hour limit is strictly enforced.

Visibility is generally good at depths of 30–60 feet (9–18 meters). The best diving is located straight out from the west side of the point. The marine life is colorful and varied; divers often report seeing bat rays, torpedo rays, schools of rockfish and a friendly harbor seal named Spot, who cruises the sandy areas between the tall rocky outcroppings. The rocky surface is covered with a carpet of sponges, anemones, starfish, barnacles, and nudibranchs. Spearfishing is strictly prohibited at Lover's Point.

The area just off the point is relatively shallow (15–20 feet, or 5–6 meters) and the bottom consists mostly of large boulders and rocks—a popular spot for monkeyface eels. You can coax these somewhat shy fish from the caves with scraps of food. Some divers have managed to get monkeyface eels to eat right out of their hands. With the aid of a dive buddy to feed the fish, underwater photographers can come away with some unusual shots. Monkeyface eels are not true eels, and so don't have large teeth.

Typical depth range	:	25–55 feet (8–16 meters)
Typical water conditions	:	Light to moderate surge
Expertise required	:	Intermediate
Access	:	Rocky shoreline, shallow rocky entry

Otter Cove is located just a few blocks from Lover's Point at the corner of Ocean View Boulevard and Sea Palm Avenue. The narrow rocky beach can be reached by climbing down a short, steep slope. The city removed the decayed wooden stairway that had been used by divers to traverse the slope, but it is planning to replace it.

Entry can be difficult here because the water is only waist deep for a long distance from the beach. If the surf is at all heavy, divers risk getting tangled in the kelp or being thrown against the jagged rocks.

When the water is calm, though, access is relatively easy and the long swim out is definitely worth the effort. Once beyond the surf line (150

The rose anemone is easily recognized by its deep-red column and white tentacles.

When the warm El Nino current moves north into Monterey, it brings with it pelagic creatures, such as these red crabs, from the waters further south.

yards, or 140 meters, from shore), the bottom drops away fairly quickly to 50 feet (15 meters). Here, you'll find large rocky pinnacles protruding from the sandy bottom, forming miniature mountains. Dense patches of small strawberry anemones, decorator crabs, cup corals, large tealia anemones, starfish, plume worms, and sea hares cling to the rocks. Purple-ringed top shells, one of Monterey's most beautiful mollusks, can be found on kelp fronds or in the beds of corynactus. It's no wonder that photographers sometimes spend an entire dive in an area that's no larger than a table top.

The reef that extends into the bay a good distance from shore and the variety of the terrain will provide an interesting dive. Without a compass, though, it's easy to lose your sense of direction. If you're beach diving, I recommend that you surface with at least 1000 psi to determine your distance and direction from shore. The kelp can get fairly thick in this area, so it is usually easier and safer to return to shore by swimming under the kelp than by trying to crawl over it at the surface.

Typical depth range   :   20–40 feet (6–12 meters)

Typical water conditions   :   Light to moderate surge, variable
                                     coastal current

Expertise required   :   Novice to intermediate

Access   :   Beach

Because the entry to Coral Street Beach is well protected, it is often used by instructors to teach novice divers, particularly when the ocean is calm. The beach is located at the corner of Coral Street and Ocean View Boulevard, where there is a natural breakwater that protects the area from swells. Parking is readily available, but there are no restroom facilities.

Purple-ringed top shells are often found feeding on the kelp fronds just below the surface of the water.

Coral Street is a good place to look for a wide variety of macro photography subjects, such as this hermit crab.

If you enter the water on the left side of the beach inside the breakwater, you'll find a wide channel that drops quickly to about 20 feet (6 meters). The flat sandy bottom is littered with old abalone shells. Unlike most dive sites along the Monterey Peninsula, Coral Street Beach lacks an abundance of marine life. But it's a terrific place for underwater photography because of the unusually clear water, which allows a lot of light to penetrate to the bottom.

Coastal currents that run parallel to the shore can get quite strong beyond the breakwater on the west side of the cove. You might find it easier to swim underwater most of the way back to the beach rather than fight the surface currents. Once inside the point, the water is usually very calm. The major drawback of Coral Street Beach is that the kelp gets very thick during the late summer and fall.

Typical depth range	:	Inner Chase Reef—40–50 feet (12–15 meters); Outer Chase Reef—40–80 feet (12–25 meters)
Typical water conditions	:	Inner Chase Reef—moderate surge with 2–4 foot (1–2 meter) swells; Outer Chase Reef—sometimes large swells with fairly strong currents
Expertise required	:	Inner Chase Reef—Intermediate, preferably with experience in strong surge; Outer Chase Reef—Intermediate to advanced
Access	:	Inner Chase Reef—long swim from Coral Street Beach, boat; Outer Chase Reef—boat

A small octopus forages for food among a clump of huge metridium anemones on Outer Chase Reef.

Chase Reef lies just north of Point Pinos at the western tip of Monterey Bay. Vulnerable to the prevailing northwesterly swells, diving this site can be treacherous during rough weather but beautiful when the winds are calm. Because of the long swim from shore—300–400 yards (276–370 meters)—most divers travel to Inner Chase Reef by boat. Too bad, because the terrain is very interesting on the way out. If you're an experienced diver and would like to try the swim (on calm days only), leave from Coral Street and head out slightly to the left. Take a surf mat with you to give your legs a rest during the long trip back to the beach. Dive boards, which are easy to launch from Coral Street, can also help get you to the outer edge of the kelp bed.

Inner Chase Reef is a series of rocky ridges with numerous crevices and caves that run parallel to shore in 40–60 feet (12–18 meters) of water. Outer Chase Reef, located near Point Pinos, has a number of dropoffs, some of which fall to 100 feet (30 meters). There is a high archway at the edge of one of these dropoffs, which is lined with white metridium anemones. The walls are completely covered with sponge, bryozoans, and colonies of anemones. This is an excellent area for macrophotography, thanks to an incredible array of nudibranchs, starfish, and other creatures which comb the bottom for food.

Be aware that the swells can get fairly large at Outer Chase Reef, especially in the afternoon. Anchors should be set securely and leave plenty of slack in the line. As always, begin your dive by swimming into the current and return with the current.

A diver swims through the kelp beds at Chase Reef. Chase Reef boasts one of the largest kelp beds to be found in the Monterey area.

Carmel Bay

Most of the dive sites in Carmel Bay are more exposed to the weather than those in Monterey Bay, so that water conditions are rougher, the surf higher, and the surge stronger. These spots also tend to be deeper, with walls dropping well below the limits for sport divers. The proximity of the Carmel Trench keeps the water a few degrees cooler than that in Monterey Bay as well, averaging 49–52 degrees Fahrenheit (9–12 degrees Celsius) at the surface and dropping as low as 46 degrees at depth. One significant benefit of the cold upwellings is that the water clarity is often substantially better in Carmel Bay than in Monterey, with visibility often exceeding 60 feet (18 meters) at the Pinnacles, Mono Lobo, Monastery Beach and Point Lobos.

DIVE SITE RATINGS

	Novice	Intermediate	Advanced
10 The Ocean Pinnacles		×	×
11 Stillwater Cove	×	×	×
12 Copper Roof House			×
13 Carmel River Beach		×	×
14 Monastery Beach			×
15 Mono Lobo		×	×
16 Point Lobos	×	×	×

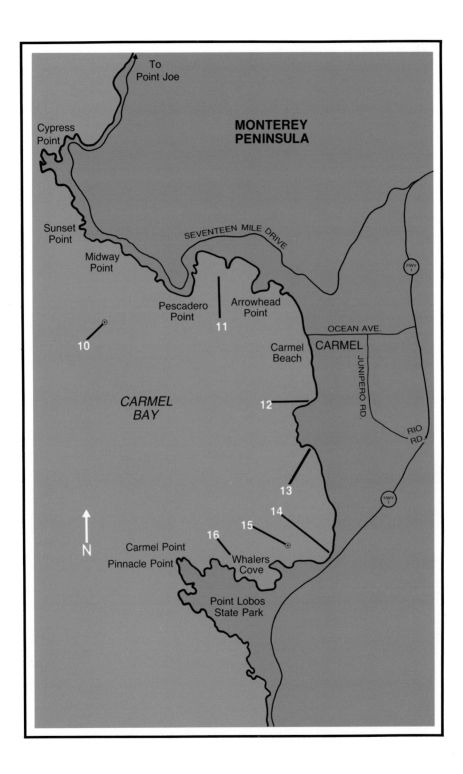

To
Point Joe

Cypress
Point

**MONTEREY
PENINSULA**

Sunset
Point

SEVENTEEN MILE DRIVE

Midway
Point

HWY
1

Pescadero
Point

Arrowhead
Point

11

OCEAN AVE.

Carmel
Beach

CARMEL

JUNIPERO RD.

*CARMEL
BAY*

12

RIO
RD.

13

HWY

14

N

15

Carmel Point

16

Pinnacle Point

Whalers
Cove

Point Lobos
State Park

Typical depth range	:	40–110 feet (12–33 meters)
Typical water conditions	:	Moderate to heavy surge, intermittent current, boat ride often rough
Expertise required	:	Advanced intermediate to advanced, good diving skills and experience in current and open-water dives
Access	:	Boat only

This is one of Monterey Peninsula's premier dive destinations. Even if you plan to do only a few dives in the Monterey area, the Ocean Pinnacles should be on your agenda.

The pinnacles are actually two separate underwater mountains about a quarter-mile apart. The inner pinnacle, which extends to within 12 feet (4 meters) of the surface, is located approximately three-quarters of a mile offshore between Pescadero Point and Cypress Point. The top of the outer pinnacle is actually a series of flat plateaus in 45–65 feet (14–19 meters) of water. Each pinnacle is like a jagged mountain peak, with steep dropoffs

Hydrocorals, found in hues of pink, orange, and lavender, are common in depths below 60 feet at the Ocean Pinnacles.

and narrow canyons falling away to depths in excess of 100 feet (30 meters). The pinnacles are marked with thick kelp beds that rise from the bottom. As a land reference point, look for a large pink house with a high tower, nicknamed "The Castle House."

The kelp, reaching upward as much as 100 feet (30 meters) on slender stalks from the reefs below, forms a thick and imposing canopy at the surface. Massive schools of blue rockfish can be found hanging motionless just beneath the kelp canopy. One of the most incredible things about this reef area is that every square inch of the surface is blanketed with colorful invertebrates. At depths of 60–90 feet (18–28 meters), there are whole colonies of pink, purple, and orange hydrocoral. This hydrozoan is usually found only on offshore reefs and pinnacles where the currents are strong, the water is clean, and there is an abundance of plankton. Photographers will find this area a miniature wonderland of nudibranchs, shrimp, barnacles, and tube worms.

The only way to reach the pinnacles is by boat. The dive charter boats operating out of Monterey make regular visits to the pinnacles. You can also make the 10-mile (16-kilometer) run from the launch ramps inside the Monterey Breakwater.

Hydrocorals are only one of many colorful and beautiful animals found in the deep recesses of underwater forests at the Ocean Pinnacles.

Typical depth range	:	20–50 feet (6–15 meters)
Typical water conditions	:	Dense kelp, calm water
Experience required	:	Novice to intermediate
Access	:	Beach, charter boats, dive boards, boat launch facility

On days when heavy seas and strong winds cancel a trip to the Pinnacles, charter boats often duck into Stillwater Cove. The substitution is a good thing for photographers, because Stillwater Cove offers an excellent opportunity to work on photos of kelp and divers. The visibility is quite good and the uneven terrain adds drama to photos. But don't underestimate the sport diving possibilities. Closer to shore, divers will find many species of fish which are thought to be native only to Southern California, such as opaleye and sheepshead.

A charter boat, one of many that operate out of Monterey Bay, anchors in the calm waters of Stillwater Cove at the northern edge of Carmel Bay.

Large shrimp can be found in large numbers on the bottom in Stillwater Cove.

When the winds kick up from the northwest, the cove turns into a glassy pond, lying protected behind the shelter of Pescadero Point. There is a public beach entry to the area plus a renovated concrete pier that's equipped with a boat hoist for launching boats. There are six parking spaces near the pier (reservations required) and additional parking at the Pebble Beach Lodge. Restroom facilities and a public telephone are also available. For more information about parking reservations and entrance and boat launch fees, contact the Pebble Beach Corporation (ask for the beach club). Also, check to see what additional equipment, if any, is required for launches.

Typical depth range	:	20–60 feet (6–18 meters)
Typical water conditions	:	Moderate to heavy surf
Expertise required	:	Advanced, with experience in surf entries and exits
Access	:	Sandy beach, dive boards

Copper Roof House is named for the green copper roof of a nearby house designed by the architect Frank Lloyd Wright. The architect built the house in the shape of a ship, fitting testament to the sometimes brutal weather that sometimes afflicts the area. I recommend that only advanced divers explore Copper Roof House. The area is located in the jaws of the northwest swells and can become quite treacherous even during the best conditions.

You can get to the beach via a stairway located at the corner of Martin Street and Scenic Drive. The stairway is often damaged by winter storms and is usually posted with signs saying it is unsafe. When conditions permit diving, you can enter the water at the south end of the wide beach and swim toward the north end of the kelp bed that surrounds the point. Schools of blue, olive, and black rockfish can be found at the edges of the kelp beds.

A submerged reef stretches in a jagged line from the point at Copper Roof to the wash rocks outside Stillwater Cove at a depth of 50–60 feet (15–18 meters). Approximately 500 yards (460 meters) offshore, the reef is broken by a number of sandy channels, a spot favored by freedivers in search of halibut and several varieties of rockfish.

Masking crabs camouflage themselves by covering their bodies with sponges, hydroids, bryozoans, tunicates, and other encrusting invertebrates, turning themselves into mobile mini-reefs.

Typical depth range	:	20–60 feet (6–18 meters)
Typical water conditions	:	Moderate surf and swells that can get rough
Expertise required	:	Intermediate to advanced, skilled in surf entries and exits
Access	:	Sandy beach

Carmel River Beach is a large sandy area located near the mouth of Carmel River. Diving conditions can be hazardous at times, so visit this area only when conditions are calm. Nevertheless, an interesting rocky reef, adequate parking, and restroom facilities make this location popular with the local divers.

Amidst the dense kelp forests you'll find ling cod, cabezon, and a variety of rockfish and other colorful marine life. While sightseers find the area satisfying, the visibility is rarely good enough for anything but close-up photography, and the selection of macro-photo subjects isn't as great here as at some other spots nearby.

Enter Carmel River Beach at the corner of Scenic Road and Ocean-view Avenue, about 1,000 feet (307 meters) from the parking lot entrance. Many divers prefer the diving at this end of the beach.

A diver swims beneath a canopy of kelp. The water is cold—about 50 degrees Fahrenheit—and visibility often reaches 60 feet (18 meters).

Typical depth range	:	30 feet (10 meters) to unlimited (submarine canyon)
Typical water conditions	:	Moderate to heavy surf and surge
Expertise required	:	Advanced, with experience in surf entries and exits
Access	:	Steep sandy beach

Monastery Beach, located on Highway 1, about four miles south of the intersection of Highway 1 and Highway 68, is one of the best-known dive sites on the Monterey Peninsula.

You can enter the water at the kelp beds at either end of the beach. The surf is generally rough in the center of the beach, and there is nothing but sandy bottom separating the kelp beds. The beach drops off sharply at Monastery, causing the surf to rise very quickly. This can make entries and exits extremely difficult except on very calm days. Even if you're an experienced diver, avoid the area when the surf is heavy. Even when the surf is only moderate, divers should enter and exit with caution. No one should dive Monastery Beach without being properly trained in surf entries and exits.

Monastery Beach can be rough, requiring a degree of skill in surf entries and exits. The scenic beauty, however, rewards the effort.

Large lemon nudibranchs are common in the shallow waters of Monastery Beach. This bright yellow dorid nudibranch is found throughout Northern and Central California.

If you enter from the north end of the beach, follow the edge of the kelp bed straight out. About 75 yards (70 meters) offshore, the bottom drops to 20–30 feet (6–9 meters). This part of the site is outstanding for macro photography despite the surge frequently encountered here.

The head of a deep submarine canyon climbs up into the bay just beyond the largest wash rock on the outer edge of a kelp bed. The bottom drops off sharply at this point, so exercise caution. And by all means, keep track of your depth and the time—it's so easy to lose track of time watching an occasional bat ray, electric ray, leopard shark, or blue shark winding its way through the kelp. And allow a sufficient reserve of air to maneuver through the kelp and get through the surf.

The south end of Monastery is more protected than the north end, making it possible to dive the site when conditions at the north end are too hazardous. Here, the bottom doesn't drop off below 50 feet (15 meters) for several hundred yards offshore, but the rocky bottom boasts excellent color and variety inside the kelp bed.

Typical depth range	:	Walls and canyons from 40–100 feet (12–30 meters)
Typical water conditions	:	Light to moderate surge, can get rough
Expertise required	:	Intermediate to advanced
Access	:	Boat

The major attraction at Mono Lobo is a series of vertical walls that drop from 40–100 feet (12–30 meters) or more. The walls are blanketed with colonies of tiny pink, lavender, and orange anemones (corynactus), orange and yellow feather duster tube worms, chestnut cowries, and starfish of every size and shape imaginable. Within the forests of kelp which rise to the surface from the walls you'll find rays, giant sunfish, harbor seals, and other large marine denizens wending their way through schools of blue rockfish.

The Mono Lobo Wall is thick with filter feeders, such as this gorgeous green anemone.

A small patch of the Mono Lobo Wall resembles an undersea Japanese garden, with delicate pink hydrocoral, fluffy tube worms, and even a cluster of strawberry anemones.

Mono Lobo is at the edge of the kelp bed midway between Whaler's Cove in Point Lobos State Park and the south end of Monastery Beach. You can get to the site by charter boat or by inflatable, but don't attempt to anchor at Mono Lobo when there is heavy swell running. When the ocean is smooth, this can be a spectacular dive spot. Morning is the best time to dive, as the water tends to be relatively calm. During the afternoon the wind and swells kick up, and the area can get pretty rough. Because the walls are almost vertical, be cognizant of the time and your depth.

Typical depth range	:	Whaler's Cove—20–50 feet (6–15 meters); Bluefish Cove—40–110 feet (12–33 meters)
Typical water conditions	:	Whaler's Cove—Usually calm with light surge; Bluefish Cove—Moderate surge, can get rough when swells increase in size
Expertise required	:	Whaler's Cove—Novice to intermediate; Bluefish Cove—Intermediate to advanced
Access	:	Concrete boat ramp at Whaler's Cove

The Point Lobos State Reserve is located about one mile south of Monastery Beach, four miles south of Carmel on Highway 1. Diving at Point Lobos is restricted to Whaler's Cove and Bluefish Cove. And because it's a state park and marine reserve, no plants or animals may be removed or

A transluscent mass of fish eggs is nestled in the arms of pink hydrocoral. The stinging hydrocoral protects the eggs from larger predators.

Point Lobos, a marine reserve, has been preserved in pristine condition by strict enforcement of the rules, which prohibit disturbing anything above or below water.

disturbed in any way. Diving in the reserve is restricted to 15 buddy teams of two to three divers. The restriction on the number of divers is enforced so that a balance can be maintained between the preservation of the underwater park's natural state and the protection of underwater recreational opportunities for the public.

As of January 1, 1990, a reservation system was initiated to allow buddy teams to reserve one of the 15 daily buddy team slots up to 28 days in advance by calling (800) 444-PARK. A nonrefundable $6 reservation fee per dive team is charged in addition to a $3 fee per vehicle. The diver making the reservation must be present in order for his or her buddy team to be admitted into the reserve. If all of the slots are not filled by 8:30 a.m., a lottery is held among those in line for the remaining spaces. Facilities at Whaler's Cove include a parking lot, restrooms, picnic tables, and freshwater rinsing hoses.

Whaler's Cove. The depths inside Whaler's Cove reach a maximum of 50 feet (15 meters) and drop to 60–70 feet (18–21 meters) just outside the cove mouth. During most of the year, the surface water in the cove is covered with a thick layer of kelp, which makes swimming difficult at best. The sandy bottom is littered with rocks and boulders. There are tunnels and caves in Coal Chute Cove, positioned directly across Whaler's Cove from the launch ramp. Shallow divers and snorkelers will find the wash rocks to the left of the cove mouth an excellent place to watch harbor seals sunbathing and sea otters foraging for food.

A maze of huge rocks and canyons brimming with docile rockfish mark the area around Bird Rock. Because the marine life is protected within the boundaries of the park, most of the fish appear almost tame. In the fall, photographers can get superb close-up shots of the ling cod which come inshore to lay their eggs.

Bluefish Cove. Many local divers consider Bluefish Cove to be the best dive site in the reserve. Certainly, there's some spectacular scenery waiting to be explored. On the east side of the cove, next to Bird Rock, canyons, small pinnacles, crevices, large boulders, and small caves shelter an assortment of rockfish, crabs, and anemones.

At the west side of the cove, solitary pinnacles rise from the flat sandy bottom 100 feet (30 meters) below the surface. In the open areas between the pinnacles you may encounter bat rays, sunfish, sea lions, schools of rockfish, and an occasional blue shark. Along the outside of the cove, stretching from Bird Rock to the middle of the cove mouth, an incredible wall extends downward from 40 feet (12 meters) to more than 100 feet (30 meters).

Large schools of blue rockfish are seen throughout the outer periphery of Bluefish Cove in Point Lobos Reserve.

Frequent upwellings bring many types of jellyfish to the surface on the outside edges of the kelp beds at Point Lobos. This large specimen of a medusa stage of the purple jellyfish is one of the most attractive of these deep-water animals.

The reef areas of Bluefish Cove are covered with a tapestry of color. It isn't uncommon to find 15 to 20 different types of nudibranchs on the outer walls during one dive. Visibility here is generally better than other dive sites around the peninsula, often exceeding 50 feet (15 meters). Some parts of Bluefish Cove are harder to access than others, and the water is deeper and frequently more rough. For these reasons, the site is most suitable for intermediate and advanced divers.

3

Diving on the North Coast of California

The north coast of California is perhaps the most scenic coastal region in the entire world. Grassy meadows, dense redwood and pine forests, and enormous waves pounding against majestic cliffs create a picturesque scene. Though always beautiful, diving conditions can change overnight. One day, calm winds and moderate surge invite sport divers to explore its underwater beauty. The next day, the same area can scare off even the most adventurous diver. Sudden swells, crashing waves, and powerful wind and rain show the inhospitable side of the north coast. But despite these periods of inclement weather, the coast holds out the lure of fascination to hundreds of divers and to abalone hunters, who flock to the area on weekends for superb hunting during the season.

Jenner-by-the-Sea, a little town located at the mouth of the Russian River, is the jumping off point for the long journey along winding roads up the coast to the north. To reach Jenner from San Francisco, take U.S. Highway 101 to the Russian River/Old River Road turnoff just north of Santa Rosa. The Old River Road joins Highway 116 at Guerneville and continues west to Jenner and the coast. You can also reach Jenner by taking the Bodega Bay turnoff on Highway 101 at Petaluma. This route joins Highway 1 just below Bodega Bay, which was the setting for Alfred Hitchcock's movie "The Birds."

North of Jenner, Highway 1 is a two-lane road cut out of the cliffs hundreds of feet above the ocean. The only thing that separates you from the steep drop to the ocean are a few guard rails on the more dangerous curves. The scenery is breathtakingly beautiful. Sheep graze the meadows on either side of the highway and, every so often, you'll come across one staring at you from the roadside or even standing in the middle of the road. And, of course, along the journey from Jenner to Fort Bragg you'll pass many excellent dive sites.

Diving for Red Abalone. The abalone is a large mollusk with a bowl-shaped shell on the top and a heavy, muscular foot on the bottom. The delicate flavor of the large foot, when properly prepared, has made this animal one of the most highly-prized catches—and highest-priced

Nudibranchs are almost as common along the North Coast as they are in Monterey. Here, a solitary hermissenda crassicornis forages along a rocky bottom. ➤

Tips on Abalone Diving

● To measure the abalone to ensure that it's large enough to be removed from the bottom, hold your gloved hand over the shell with your fingers and thumb spread. If you can't see shell extending beyond either side of your fingers, from the tip of your thumb to the tip of your little finger, it's probably too small. You can also measure the abalone by using a properly marked ab iron. But remember that if you touch an abalone, it will clamp down on the rocky bottom, making it very difficult to remove.

● Once you find an abalone that is larger than 7 inches (18 centimeters), slowly insert the end of the ab iron between the rock and the mollusk's foot (2–3 inches, or 5–8 centimeters, should be sufficient). Pull the handle up and away from the rock so that the end of the iron presses against the rock, and the middle of the iron pries the side of the shell away from the rock. Be careful not to cut the abalone in case you discover upon removing it that it's too small.

● On days when it's particularly calm, look for areas that are normally rough and filled with white water. Your chances of finding large abs will be greater because these areas aren't dived as heavily as more protected areas.

● Abalone are most often found under ledges and in cracks and crevices. When you're diving in relatively shallow water, don't neglect the hard-to-get-to areas. Try not to fight the surge; if you relax and go where the water takes you, you'll be able to extend your bottom time. The more energy you exert underwater, the faster you will use up your air.

The famed California red abalone is seen here in its natural habitat. Often, its shell is covered with the same growth as the rocks it clings to, making it very hard to spot. Look for the small holes in the shell or a fringe of the black mantle.

seafood dishes—on the West Coast. Red abalone (Haliotis Rufescens) are still fairly abundant in shallow water along the rocky areas of the north coast from Jenner to Mendocino. You can usually find "abs" in water that's less than 40 feet (12 meters) deep. Abalone feed on kelp, so if you find a thick, plush kelp bed, you can bet on finding one or more of these culinary delicacies as well.

A word of caution about the regulations on diving for abalone on the north coast. Sport divers are not permitted to take abalone while wearing scuba tanks; free diving is the only method permitted for hunting abalone. What's more, the maximum number of abalone that can be removed each day is currently four per person. And you're not allowed to remove a red abalone that's less than 7 inches (18 centimeters) long, determined by measuring the maximum diameter of the shell. The abalone season in this area extends from April 1 to June 30, and from August 1 to November 30.

Sonoma County

Most of the dive spots in Sonoma County are located between Fort Ross Reef Campground (11 miles north of Jenner) and Stewart's Point, approximately 28 miles north of Jenner. Free diving is the most popular activity among sport divers here because, with the exception of a few protected coves, access to most of the good game spots requires a long hike with your gear. There are, however, several spots in Sonoma County which are easily accessible. Timber Cove, Stillwater Cove, and Gerstle Cove (in Salt Point State Park) are all fairly well protected from northwest swells and have launching areas suitable for small inflatables. Timber Cove has a small dive store and the best launching facility in the area. There are also a number of good reefs and coves outside Timber Cove, including Cemetery Reef, which can only be reached by boat.

Sea Ranch is a private development in the northern section of Sonoma County. Sea Ranch has four public accesses along Highway 1. These accesses provide parking and require a long walk to the coast, but it is usually true that the harder it is to get to an area, the larger and more abundant the abalone.

DIVE SITE RATINGS

	Novice – Intermediate	Intermediate	Advanced
17 Fort Ross Reef Campgrounds		×	×
18 Ft. Ross State Park	×	×	×
19 Timber Cove		×	×
20 Cemetery Reef			×
21 Stillwater Cove	×	×	×
22 Ocean Cove		×	×
23 Salt Point State Park	×	×	×

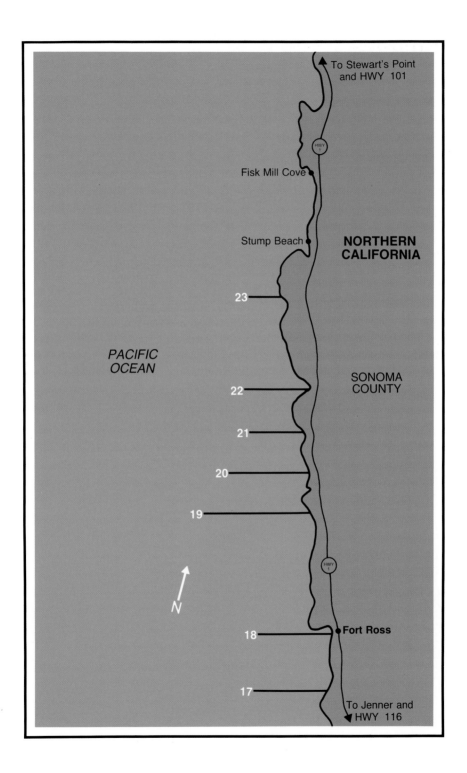

To Stewart's Point
and HWY 101

Fisk Mill Cove

Stump Beach

**NORTHERN
CALIFORNIA**

23

*PACIFIC
OCEAN*

22

SONOMA
COUNTY

21

20

19

N

18   **Fort Ross**

17

To Jenner and
HWY 116

Typical depth range	:	10–50 feet (3–15 meters)
Typical water conditions	:	Moderate to heavy surf and surge
Expertise required	:	Intermediate to advanced
Access	:	Beach, dive board

Fort Ross Reef Campground (formerly Red Barn State Park) is located 11 miles (18 kilometers) north of Jenner on Highway 1. There are two access roads from the main gate. One allows you to park on the bluffs that rise some 60 feet (18 meters) above the main beach. The other, which cuts through a ravine, takes you almost to the shore. The ravine entry is less demanding in that you won't have to carry your gear up and down the cliffs. However, the bluffs are much closer to the best diving area, which is located off the south beach.

The abalone are relatively small in this area, but the spearfishing is good. The bottom is very shallow off the beach; it's less than 15 feet (5 meters) deep as far as a quarter-mile offshore. On the south end of the beach, past the pinnacles which rise above the surface, the bottom is 10–20 feet (3–6 meters), though crevices in the bottom make some areas much deeper. Here you'll find schools of blue and black rockfish, kelp greenlings,

Fort Ross Reef Campground is the southernmost of the popular Sonoma County dive spots. It can be exciting; however, visibility is sometimes impaired by runoff from the mouth of the Russian River.

A large metridium anemone hangs upside down in a rocky crevice. The anemones seem to like the colder waters of Northern California.

deep-water reds, ling cod, olive rockfish, and surf perch. This area is somewhat protected from the vicious storms coming out of the northwest. However, the runoff from the mouth of the Russian River frequently reduces visibility.

This site is rarely visited by scuba divers but is a popular site among free divers.

Typical depth range	:	10–60 feet (3–18 meters)
Typical water conditions	:	Calm, well protected from northwest storms
Expertise required	:	Novice to intermediate
Access	:	Beach, dive board, boat

The remains of the *Pomona*, a 225-foot (70-meter) deluxe passenger freighter which broke up and sank at Fort Ross in 1907, are strewn over a large area. The ship, constructed in 1888, went down while making the trek between San Francisco and Eureka. Divers still occasionally find portholes, fittings, parts of the huge mast, winches, boilers, or other pieces of the ship, but do not remove anything: The entire wreck is within the boundaries of the state park and is protected.

Fort Ross is located on Highway 1, a mile above the entrance to Fort Ross Reef Campgrounds, 12 miles north of Jenner. In 1812 Russian fur trappers built a fort and trading settlement on this site. The fort has since been completely restored and is a major tourist attraction. For divers, Fort Ross Cove offers calm water when other dive areas along the north coast

Abalone divers check their haul of the delicious shellfish after a morning dive at Fort Ross.

An abalone diver, ab iron in hand, floats at the surface before making a free dive. Abalone cannot be taken with tanks on the California north coast.

are weathered out by rough water and northwest swells. However, the visibility is usually not as good as it is elsewhere on the coast.

There are actually two coves at Fort Ross, but the north cove and its northern points offer the best diving. There's a large wash rock in the middle of the cove and, lying directly in line with the wash rock and the beach is the *Pomona*. The wreck is scattered in 15–25 feet (5–8 meters) of water.

Beyond the wash rock, the bottom drops quickly to 40–50 feet (12–15 meters). Sediment covers just about everything except for white metridium anemones on the rocky reef. The best abalone diving is around the northern point, but the water here is often too rough to dive. Another good place for abalone is around a rock pile on the north side of the beach where the water is only 10 feet (3 meters) deep and is usually calm.

Typical depth range	:	10–40 feet (3–12 meters)
Typical water conditions	:	Light to moderate surf inside the cove, protected from northwest swells
Expertise required	:	Intermediate or novice accompanied by an advanced diver
Access	:	Beach, dive boards, boat launch facility

Timber Cove is located about two miles north of Fort Ross and 13 miles (21 kilometers) north of Jenner on Highway 1. The main attraction is a large cove surrounded by high cliffs, which can be reached only by driving down a steep dirt road located on private property. Timber Cove Boat Landing offers numerous amenities including hot showers, washers and

Red abalone can still be found in large numbers in the shallow waters off Sonoma. Abalone feed on kelp, so they're usually most plentiful in areas where there are healthy kelp beds.

dryers, bait, tackle, a small dive store, overnight camping, and a boat launch that can accommodate boats up to 18 feet (5.5 meters) in length. The owners charge beach access and boat launch fees.

The inside of the cove is generally protected from the prevailing ocean swells. The resulting onslaught of sport divers has driven away many of the game fish and large abalone that once thrived here. You can still find a plentiful supply of abalone most of the year in the dense kelp beds to the north and south of the cove. These are also good spots for tank diving, spearfishing, and general sightseeing.

It's tempting to swim all the way out around the north point to dive in the cluster of wash rocks, but this should only be attempted on exceptionally calm days. The boat launching facility allows access to many areas to the north of Timber Cove which can't be reached from shore.

Harbor seals are frequent visitors to the main beach. You'll often see a young seal frolicking in the shallow waters waiting for handouts from divers who are cleaning fish, or just checking out the human activity on the beach. The seals that swim within the sheltered coves to the north of Timber Cove are a bit more aggressive. They've been known to steal fish off the stringers of divers who are spearfishing.

A free diver surfaces through the kelp with an abalone.

Typical depth range	:	30–70 feet (10–21 meters)
Typical water conditions	:	Moderate to heavy swells; currents can be strong
Expertise required	:	Advanced with open water skills
Access	:	Boat only

Cemetery Reef, located north of Timber Cove, is a one-mile (1.6-kilometer) ridge running parallel to shore. The reef was named after a small cemetery which overlooks the ocean. The best diving is around the L-shaped plateau which lies about 400 yards (370 meters) offshore, midway between Timber Cove and Stillwater Cove. The top of the reef, in 20–30 feet (6–10 meters) of water, is carpeted with a dense layer of algae, along with strands of bull kelp. Large abalone are abundant on the top of the reef and are well within the range of free divers.

The sides of the reef are nearly vertical, dropping to a jumble of massive boulders and rocks at 40–70 feet (12–21 meters). Brightly colored encrusting sponge, colonies of corynactus, large acorn barnacles, and

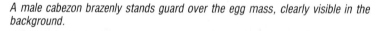

A male cabezon brazenly stands guard over the egg mass, clearly visible in the background.

A red abalone, with mantel raised, forages for food. Abalone feed on kelp.

metridium anemones cover the walls, making them a spectacular backdrop for photographing divers and fish. Expect to find large ling cod, cabezon, and sea trout making their way through the maze of cracks and crevices formed by the boulders and rocks.

The visibility is often better here than in areas closer to the shore because of currents which can be strong. Be sure to check that your boat anchor is secure and leave plenty of slack in the line.

Typical depth range	:	10–40 feet (3–12 meters)
Typical water conditions	:	Often calm inside the cove
Expertise required	:	Novice accompanied by an advanced diver
Access	:	Beach, dive board, small inflatables

As you may have guessed from the name, this site is well protected from strong currents and wave action. In fact, Stillwater Cove is just about the only place where you can get into the water during high seas, a major reason why this cove and several others in the area are used for basic scuba instruction. The middle of the cove is marked by fairly rugged and barren terrain, so you'll want to head for the northern or southern points

An abalone diver floats among bull kelp at the surface, waiting to take another free dive.

A diver gears up at Stillwater Cove in Sonoma County (not to be confused with Stillwater Cove in Monterey Bay). The cove provides one of the few sheltered entry points along the rugged North Coast.

of the cove. Visibility is not usually good in the areas closest to the beach, but the water begins to clear about 75–100 yards (70–97 meters) from shore. For good tank diving head straight out from the beach until the bottom drops to 50 feet (15 meters). Because this cove gets such heavy traffic, very few legal-size abalone can be found in water less than 20 feet (6 meters) deep.

Small inflatables can be launched across the pebble beach. Dive boards are also used to reach areas that are beyond swimming distance. Spearfishermen have taken good-size ling cod in the outer areas of the cove, especially during the fall when lings leave deeper water to spawn on the shallow, rocky reefs.

Typical depth range	:	10–50 feet (3–15 meters)
Typical water conditions	:	Moderate to heavy swells, although can be extremely calm at times
Expertise required	:	Intermediate to advanced
Access	:	Beach, dive boards, small inflatables, steep paths

Ocean Cove is on private property. However, you can get into the area by paying a "trespass" fee at the Ocean Cove grocery store, located across the road from the entrance gate. Facilities include campsites and toilets, but no running water.

The entrance to Ocean Cove is located at a sharp curve in the road one mile north of Stillwater Cove on Highway 1. Once inside the main gate you'll see a fork in the road. The right fork leads to a bluff that overlooks the main beach. Follow the left fork to reach the cliffs at the south point of

Ocean Cove, a popular entry point, is privately owned. Divers must pay an access fee at the grocery store across from the main entrance. There's plenty of room for cookouts and camping on the bluffs overlooking the ocean.

An abalone diver penetrates a deep "glory hole" off the southern tip of Ocean Cove. Here, the diver finds a prized abalone with a shell in excess of 10 inches.

the cove. There's also a road that leads down to a rocky beach where you can launch small inflatables.

The best diving begins at the large wash rock near the south point of the cove. The path that gets you there is steep and covered with loose sand, making the task of hauling gear up and down the cliff that much harder. But your efforts will be rewarded, especially if you're hunting for abalone or fish. The south wall at the point and the area just outside of the point are excellent spots for abalone. You can find "glory holes," small pockets in the bottom filled with abalone, in less than 15 feet (5 meters) of water. Some of the deep holes in this area drop below 50 feet (15 meters). The kelp bed around the southern point is dense most of the year and may pose a problem for free divers, so be careful.

As for the north point of the cove, you'll find excellent spearfishing on the reef just outside the cove. Plan on getting to the site by boat or dive board; it's definitely too far to swim from shore. Because Ocean Cove is exposed to northwest swells, the water can get very rough.

Typical depth range	:	Gerstle Cove—15–90 feet (5–28 meters;
		South Gerstle Cove—10–50 feet (3–15 meters)
Typical water conditions	:	Gerstle Cove—calm to moderate surge;
		South Gerstle Cove—moderate to heavy surge, sometimes large swells
Expertise required	:	Gerstle Cove—novice to intermediate;
		South Gerstle Cove—intermediate
Access	:	Gerstle Cove—Beach, dive boards, small inflatables;
		South Gerstle Cove—Beach, steep path

Gerstle Cove and South Gerstle Cove are the most popular dive sites in Salt Point State Park, located about one mile north of Ocean Cove on Highway 1. The bottom terrain of Gerstle Cove, an underwater reserve, is

Divers use the rocky beach at Gerstle Cove as a protected access point to dive the reserve inside Salt Point State Park.

Squatter's rights: This hermit crab warily eyes the photographer from the safety of an abandoned top shell.

rugged. At the mouth of the cove, the water is about 50 feet (15 meters) deep, then drops off quickly to 80 feet (25 meters) or more. Photographers will find the cove a good place for macrophotography, as there are large numbers of nudibranchs, chitons, strawberry anemones, a variety of starfish, and other creatures. The extensive kelp beds outside the cove are also good spots for abalone hunting, sightseeing, and spearfishing.

Water conditions at South Gerstle Cove are usually rougher than in the reserve, but access is still fairly easy, except on days when the ocean is rough. The best place for abalone diving here is on the outside of the north point in 15–30 feet (5–10 meters) of water.

The facilities at Salt Point State Park include restrooms, outdoor showers, changing rooms, and a fish-cleaning station. There are many campsites at Salt Point on both sides of Highway 1. A paved road leads down to the beach at Gerstle, where divers can launch small boats or dive boards. This is also a good entry point for swimming out with surf mats or floats.

Two other coves have recently been added to Salt Point State Park—Stump Beach and Fisk Mill Cove. Both areas are exposed to the elements, creating dangerous surf and limiting visibility. On calm days the diving, especially for abalone, can be quite good along the northern points of these coves.

Mendocino County

Mendocino is even farther away from the more heavily populated areas in northern and central California, so it doesn't attract as many divers as sites in Sonoma County. If you've got the time, and don't mind a scenic ride into some of the farther reaches of northern California, you might visit Anchor Bay, Navarro River, Albion, Van Damme, and Russian Gulch. All of these locations are located on Highway 1 and they're easy to find. The nearby coves and reefs can be accessed by boat or dive board from all these points.

Mendocino County also offers plenty of tourist attractions, the most popular being the bed and breakfast inns, which provide romantic retreats for sport divers and tourists alike. If you'd like to take in more of the extraordinary scenery of the area, consider a ride on the old narrow gauge Skunk Railroad, which travels between Willits and the coast. You can sit back, relax, take in the beauty of the redwood forests, and also learn a little bit about the history of California's logging industry.

The list of tourist attractions is seemingly endless. If time permits, you'll undoubtedly want to tour one of the nearby wineries, go whale watching, hike through pygmy forests and fern grottos, or simply browse a few of Mendocino's quaint shops.

It's always a good idea to make reservations for lodging in advance. In keeping with the untouched beauty and rural setting in Mendocino County, the lodging facilities are limited. At some times of the year it may be difficult to find camper hookups, a motel room, or space at a campsite. Make your reservations early, and check on the weather and water conditions before you head north.

DIVE SITE RATINGS

	Novice–Intermediate	Intermediate	Advanced
24 Anchor Bay		×	×
25 Navarro River Beach		×	×
26 Albion		×	×
27 Van Damme State Park	×	×	×
28 Russian Gulch	×	×	×

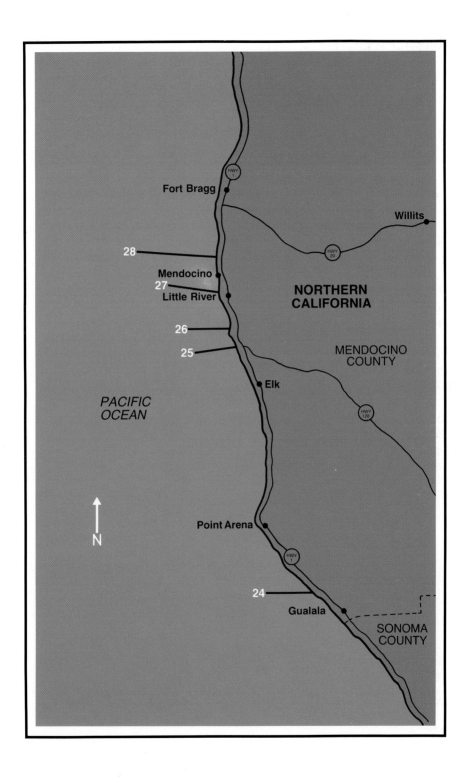

Typical depth range	:	10–60 feet (3–18 meters)
Typical water conditions	:	Moderate to rough surf
Expertise required	:	Intermediate to advanced
Access	:	Beach, dive boards, boat launching across beach

Anchor Bay is a privately owned campground and beach access located in Gualala on Highway 1. Facilities include campsites (most with electricity and water), restrooms, and showers. Information about rates and reservations can be obtained by calling 707–884–4222. With a grocery store, laundromat, and several restaurants nearby, Anchor Bay is ideal for family camping.

The best diving is on the north end of the beach, which is three-quarters of a mile (1.2 kilometers) long. During the summer and fall months, you can have a small-to-medium sized inflatable launched across the sand at the north end of the cove. From there, a channel between the north wall of the cove and several wash rocks leads to an area called Fish Rock, just outside the point. Beyond Fish Rock, the bottom drops steeply

Fish Rock, at the north point of Anchor Bay, has collected its share of shipwrecks over the years, and bits of wreckage make it interesting diving. Sail Rock is just beyond the mouth of the bay.

An abalone diver descends through the underwater forest of bull kelp searching for abalone on the rocky bottom.

to a plateau in about 40 feet (12 meters) of water, then drops off into progressively deeper water across a series of cuts that run roughly north to south. Schools of blue and black rockfish can be found here, along with cabezon and ling cod. The bottom is host to platoons of starfish, box crabs, nudibranchs and, in 60 feet (18 meters) of water, white metridium anemones.

Typical depth range	:	5–35 feet (2–11 meters)
Typical water conditions	:	Moderate surf, do not dive when rough
Expertise required	:	Intermediate to advanced
Access	:	Beach, dive boards, small boats

Navarro River is primarily visited by free divers. Straight out from the center of the beach is a wide, shallow shelf which extends from shore out to an offshore reef. In the shallow water, from 50 to 75 yards (46–70 meters) from shore, the ocean water mixes with fresh water from the Navarro River, which causes extremely poor visibility. Outside of this area, a series of rock piles in 10–20 feet (3–6 meters) of water are home to an a host of abalone. Toward the north side of the beach is another reef where

Jewel-like top shells are common on rocky surfaces and in kelp beds throughout Northern California.

Solitary rose anemones, which grow up to ten inches in diameter, are also common sights in Sonoma and Mendocino waters.

large 9-inch (23-centimeter) abalone are common. Outside of this north breaker, the walls of isolated pinnacles drop vertically to about 20 feet (6 meters). Finger canyons, which extend toward the open ocean, drop down to 35 feet (11 meters). The north wall, above the mouth of the river, is another prime abalone spot, as well as for rock scallops and large urchins. Outside the wash rocks to the north side of the beach near the rock called "Navarro Arch" is an area where large schools of blue and black rock fish are common.

Navarro River is located at the junction of Highway 1 and Highway 128 in Mendocino County, at the mouth of the Navarro River. Camping is allowed near the beach on the south side of the river mouth.

Typical depth range	:	10–60 feet (3–18 meters)
Typical water conditions	:	Calm to moderate swells inside the cove; moderate to rough swells outside
Expertise required	:	Intermediate
Access	:	Beach, dive boards, small boats

Access to the diving at Albion Cove is primarily by boat. There is an island at the north end of the cove which breaks up incoming swells from the northwest. This keeps the north end of the cove fairly calm. North of the point, the water is often rough, but there are protected coves and channels on the inside which are filled with abalone, fish, and plant life.

This colorful Hilton's nudibranch climbs among the branches of this pink coralline algae.

In the center of the boat channel, just outside of the bridge, is a group of rock piles in 20–30 feet (6–10 meters) of water. The piles have an abundance of abalone but are dangerous for divers due to the boat traffic. The center of the cove slopes gradually toward deeper water and has a sand bottom.

On the south side of the cove, scuba divers will find large boulders, cracks, and crevices in 30–60 feet (10–18 meters) of water. This area is also popular with spearfishermen as it attracts numerous blue and black rockfish and cabezon. Several large anchors in the area attest to presence of shipwrecks as well.

Albion Cove, viewed from Highway 1 just north of the bridge over the Albion River, is a small, well-protected natural harbor. There are good dive sites along both points of the cove.

Typical depth range	:	5–50 feet (2–15 meters)
Typical water conditions	:	Calm to moderate swells inside the cove; moderate to rough swells outside
Expertise required	:	Novice to intermediate
Access	:	Beach, dive boards, small boats

Four miles north of Albion, in the town of Little River, is Van Damme State Park, which offers the most protected access in Mendocino County. It's well equipped too, and facilities include campsites, restrooms, running water, and showers. One major attraction of the park is a large fern-filled canyon. For reservations at the campground call the park at 707–937–5855 or the Department of Parks and Recreation in Sacramento at 916–445–8828.

The beach is directly across Highway 1 from the park entrance. Directly in front of the beach, boulders scattered in the shallow water are home to an impressive variety of marine life, including some abalone.

On the south side of the cove are two large, rocky islands called Top Hat and Key Hole. The dropoffs on the outside of these islands and the

The large, attractive campground just across the road from this beach has made Van Damme State Park one of the most popular North Coast dive sites.

A school of blue rockfish swims beneath a canopy of kelp.

rocky fingers on the north side of the cove provide good diving on days when the surf isn't too heavy. If you have a small boat or a dive board, you may want to explore the numerous coves to the south. These are well protected from weather and offer caves and tunnels. The water is generally clear in these coves.

Typical depth range	:	10–40 feet (3–12 meters)
Typical water conditions	:	Large protected cove, slight to moderate surge inside the cove, can be heavy outside
Expertise required	:	Novice to intermediate
Access	:	Beach, dive boards, small boats with sand wheels

Russian Gulch State Park is on Highway 1, 10 miles (16.5 kilometers) south of Fort Bragg and just north of the town of Mendocino. The park offers family camp sites, restrooms, hot showers, and some of the most spectacular scenery on the north coast. Reservations can be obtained by calling the park directly at 707–937–5804 or the Department of Parks and Recreation at 916–445–8828.

At Russian Gulch, divers can launch inflatables across the flat, sandy beach inside the protected cove. Even when the water is rough outside the cove, good diving can be had around the rocks on the south side of the inlet.

Spanish shawl nudibranchs are fairly common in shallow water at Russian Gulch.

Small boats can be launched over the protected sandy beach and into the main cove. Most divers enter the water in the main cove and dive just off shore or in the adjoining coves to the north and south.

Legal 7-inch (18-centimeter) abalone are quite plentiful here, although there are very few abalone that are much bigger than that. In recent years, the Central California Council of Diving Clubs has built several underwater habitats here and restocked the cove with baby abalone.

Novice and intermediate divers should stay away from the north point, which is generally plagued with heavy swells and surge. When the ocean is rough, the north isn't diveable at all. However, on the south side of the main cove are a group of small wash rocks. Free divers can almost always get their limit of abalone here, even when the sea is rough. This spot is also good for photography, as the rocky crevices are filled with nudibranchs, sponges, anemones, and rock scallops.

Safety

This section discusses common hazards, including dangerous marine animals, and emergency procedures in case of a diving accident. Refer to your first aid manual or emergency diving accident manual for the diagnosis or treatment of serious medical problems.

DAN

The **Divers Alert Network (DAN)**, a membership association of individuals and organizations sharing a common interest in diving safety, operates a **24-hour national hotline—(919) 684-8111** (collect calls are accepted in an emergency). DAN does not directly provide medical care, however, the network does provide advice on early treatment, evacuation, and hyperbaric treatment of diving related injuries. Additionally, DAN provides diving safety information to members to help prevent accidents. Membership is $40 a year and offers:

- the DAN *Underwater Diving Accident Manual*, which describes symptoms of and first aid for the major diving-related injuries;
- emergency room physician guidelines for drugs and i.v. fluids;
- a membership card listing diving-related symptoms on one side and DAN's emergency and nonemergency phone numbers on the other;
- one tank decal and three small equipment decals with DAN's logo and emergency number;
- a newsletter, "Alert Diver," which describes diving medicine and safety information in layman's language and contains articles for professionals, case histories, and medical questions related to diving.

Special membership for dive stores, dive clubs, and corporations is also available. The DAN manual can be purchased for $4 from the Administrative Coordinator, National Divers Alert Network, Duke University medical Center, Box 3823, Durham, NC 27710.

DAN divides the U.S. into 7 regions, each coordinated by a specialist in diving medicine who has access to the skilled hyperbaric chambers in his region. Nonemergency or information calls are connected to the DAN office and information number, (919) 684–2948. This number can be dialed directly, Monday–Friday, between 9 a.m. and 5 p.m. Eastern Standard time. Chamber status can change frequently making this kind of information dangerous if obsolete at the time of an emergency. Instead, divers should contact DAN as soon as a diving emergency is suspected. All divers should have comprehensive medical insurance and check to make sure that hyperbaric treatment and air ambulance services are covered internationally.

Diving is a safe sport and there are very few accidents compared to the number of divers and number of dives made each year. But when the infrequent injury does occur, DAN is ready to help. DAN, originally 100% federally funded, is now largely supported by the diving public. Membership in DAN or purchase of DAN manuals or decals provides divers with useful safety information and provides DAN with necessary operating funds. Donations to DAN are tax deductible as DAN is a legal non-profit public service organization.

Emergency Services

In any emergency your simplest and quickest contact for help is to dial **911**. The following numbers can also be called for help:

Monterey Peninsula

Hospitals:

MONTEREY COMMUNITY
HOSPITAL
(408) 624–5319
23625 Holman Way
Monterey, CA

Recompression Facilities:

DIVERS ALERT
NETWORK (DAN)
(919) 684-8111 (Collect calls are accepted in an emergency.)

Other Emergency Numbers:

MONTEREY U.S. COAST
GUARD
(408) 647-7300
PACIFIC GROVE MARINE
RESCUE PATROL
(408) 648-3110

MONTEREY GROUP SEARCH
AND RESCUE
(408) 647-7300

California North Coast

Hospitals:

MENDOCINO COAST HOSPITAL
(707) 961–1234
700 River Dr.
Fort Bragg, CA

REDWOOD COAST MEDICAL
SERVICES
(707) 884–4005, 785–2315
46900 Ocean Dr.
Gualala, CA

Recompression Facilities:

DIVERS ALERT NETWORK (DAN)
(919) 684–8111 (Collect calls are accepted in an emergency.)

EMERGENCY (919) 684-8111
NON-EMERGENCY   INFO
(919) 684-2948

Other Emergency Numbers:

UKIAH AREA SEARCH AND
RESCUE
(707) 463-4411 Answering Machine

FORT BRAGG AREA SEARCH
AND RESCUE
(800) 621-8299 Answering Machine

Diver Guidelines for Protecting Reefs*

1. Maintain proper buoyancy control and avoid over-weighting.
2. Use correct weight belt position to stay horizontal, i.e., raise the belt above your waist to elevate your feet/fins, and move it lower toward your hips to lower them.
3. Use your tank position in the backpack as a balance weight, i.e., raise your backpack on the tank to lower your legs, and lower the backpack on the tank to raise your legs.
4. Watch for buoyancy changes during a dive trip. During the first couple of days, you'll probably breathe a little harder and need a bit more weight than the last few days.
5. Be careful about buoyancy loss at depth; the deeper you go the more your wet suit compresses, and the more buoyancy you lose.
6. Photographers must be extra careful. Cameras and equipment affect buoyancy. Changing f-stops, framing a subject, and maintaining position for a photo often conspire to prohibit the ideal "no-touch" approach on a reef. So, when you must use "holdfasts," choose them intelligently.
7. Avoid full leg kicks when working close to the bottom and when leaving a photo scene. When you inadvertently kick something, stop kicking! Seems obvious, but some divers either semi-panic or are totally oblivious when they bump something.
8. When swimming in strong currents, be extra careful about leg kicks and handholds.
9. Attach dangling gauges, computer consoles, and octopus regulators. They are like miniature wrecking balls to a reef.
10. Never drop boat anchors onto a reef.

---

* Condensed from "Diver Guidelines" by Chris Newbert© Oceanica 1991. Reprinted with permission of Oceanica and Chris Newbert. If you are interested in more information or in helping Oceanica preserve our ocean realm, please write to Oceanica, 342 West Sunset, San Antonio, Texas 78209, USA.

Appendix

This list is included as a service to the reader. The publisher has made every effort to make this list complete at the time the book was printed. This list does not constitute an endorsement of these operators and dive shops.

Dive Services

DIVE BOAT OPERATIONS

Beach Hopper II
Marin Skin Diving
(415) 479-4332
30 foot boat, 12 divers

Cypress Sea
Cypress Charters
(408) 244-4433
50 foot boat, 20 divers

Delphi
Scubaventures
(408) 476-5201
28 foot boat, 6 divers

Navillus
Sun Tan Charters
(408) 375-9895
32 foot boat, 6 divers

Scuba Do
Lee Van Brunt
(408) 633-6178

Silver Prince
Twin Otters
(408) 394-4235
40 foot boat, 14 divers

Xeno
Sunstar Aquatics
(408) 426-7376
38 foot boat, 6 divers
open water shark cage
dives available

BOAT RENTALS

Club Nautico
(408) 373-4448
22 1/2 foot Hydro Sport boats
14 foot Yukon inflatable
boats

DIVE STORES

Adventure Sports
303 Potrero #15
Santa Cruz, CA 95060
(408) 458-3648

American Aquatic
Adventures
1104 Scenic Drive
Modesto, CA 95350
(209) 578-0515

Anchor Shack
5775 Pacheco Blvd.
Pacheco, CA 94553
(415) 825-4960

Anderson's Skin and
Scuba
541 Oceana Blvd.
Pacifica, CA 94044
(415) 355-3050

Any Water Sports
4855 Hopyard Rd. #C8
Pleasanton, CA 94566
(415) 463-3640

Any Water Sports
1130 Saratoga Ave.
San Jose, CA 95129
(408) 244-4433

Aqua Divers Inc.
300 Carriage Square
Yuba City, CA 95991
(916) 671-3483

Aqua Sports
2436 E. Terrace
Fresno, CA 93703
(209) 224-0744

Aqua Tech Scuba Center
1144 S. Main St.
Manteca, CA 95336
(209) 825-6520

Aquarius Dive Shop
2240 Del Monte Ave.
Monterey, CA 93940
(408) 375-1933

Aquarius II Dive Shop
32 Cannery Row
Coast Guard Pier
Monterey, CA 93940
(408) 375-6605

Bamboo Reef
584 - 4th Street
San Francisco, CA 94107
(415) 362-6694

Bamboo Reef
614 Lighthouse Ave.
Monterey, CA 93940
(408) 372-1685

Baxman's Bait & Tackle
884 Bodega Ave.
Petaluma, CA 94952
(707) 763-0930

Blue Water Scuba
722 Renz Lane
Gilroy, CA 95020
(408) 848-6864

Bob's Dive Shop
4374 N. Blackstone Ave.
Fresno, CA 93726
(209) 225-3483

Cal School of Diving
1750 6th Street
Berkeley, CA 94710
(415) 524-3248

Chico Dive Center
3881 Benatar Way
Chico, CA 95928
(916) 343-2431

Clearwater Oceansports
1275 Hwy. 1
Bodega Bay, CA 94923
(707) 875-3054

Dive Quest Dive Shop
2875 Glascock Street
Oakland, CA 94601
(415) 535-2415

Divers Dock
696 Auzerais Ave.
San Jose, CA 95125
(408) 298-9915

Diving Fanta Seas
1125 B. Arnold Dr., Suite 151
Martinez, CA 94553
(415) 229-3483

Diving Center of Santa Rosa
2696 Santa Rosa Ave.
Santa Rosa, CA 95401
(707) 527-8527

Dolphin Scuba
1530 El Camino
Sacramento, CA 95815
(916) 929-8188

Fish and Dive Shop
3590 Peralta Blvd.
Fremont, CA 94539
(415) 794-3474

Fremont Dive Center
41463 Albrae Street
Fremont, CA 94538
(415) 657-1004

Harbor Dive Center
200 Harbor Drive
Sausalito, CA 94965
(415) 331-0904

Lodi Skin Diving
430 W. Lockford St.
Lodi, CA 95240
(209) 333-2343

Marin Skin Diving
3765 Redwood Highway
San Rafael, CA 94903
(415) 479-4332

Mother Lode Dive Shop
2020 H Street
Sacramento, CA 95814
(916) 446-4041

Napa Gun and Dive Exchange
950 Randolph Street
Napa, CA 94559
(707) 255-3900

Nautilus Diving & Sports Center
4930 Pacific Street
Rocklin, CA 95677-2412
(916) 624-3483

North Coast Scuba
J. Baker True Value Hardware
P.O. Box 589
38820 Coast Highway
Gualala, CA 95445
(707) 884-3534

Ocean Odyssey
130 G Street
Davis, CA 95616
(916) 758-DIVE

Olympic Scuba School
2999 N. Main St.
Walnut Creek, CA 94596
(415) 933-6045

Original Steele's
1500 Monument Blvd.,
Suite F1-5
Concord, CA 94520
(415) 682-5082

Original Steele's
60th St. & Telegraph Ave.
Oakland, CA 94609
(415) 655-4344

Original Steele's
1334 Howe Ave.
Sacramento, CA 95825
(916) 923-5500

Pacific Marine Engineering
508 Myrtle Ave.
Eureka, CA 95501
(707) 442-9206

Pacific Offshore Divers
1195 Branham Lane
San Jose, CA 95118
(408) 265-3483

Peninsula Diving Center
1015 West El Camino Real
Mt. View, CA 94040
(415) 965-2241

Pinnacles Dive Shop
2112 Armory Drive
Santa Rosa, CA 95401
(707) 542-3100

Pinnacles Dive Store
875 Grant Ave.
Novato, CA 94945
(415) 897-9962

Rohnert Park Dive Center
5665 "B" Redwood Dr.
Rohnert Park, CA 94928
(707) 584-2323

Scuba Cal USA
15 Tennessee St.
Vallejo, CA 94590
(707) 642-9320

Scuba Discoveries
651 Howard Street
San Francisco, CA 94105
(415) 777-DIVE

Scuba Discoveries
965 Brewster
Redwood City, CA 94063
(415) 369-3483

Scuba Sports
8430 Auburn Blvd.
Citrus Heights, CA 95610
(916) 961-8707

Scuba Town
2631 N. Main Street
Walnut Creek, CA 94596
(415) 939-3483

Scuba Unlimited
4000 Pimlico Dr., #114
Pleasanton, CA 94588
(415) 686-0493

Scuba World
8525 Madison Ave.
Fair Oaks, CA 95628
(916) 961-7962

ScubaVentures
2222 E. Cliff Dr.
Santa Cruz, CA 95062
(408) 476-5201

Sea Horse Scuba Center
508 Couch St.
Vallejo, CA 94540
(707) 552-8898

Sports Cove Dive Shop
1410 E. Monte Vista
Vacaville, CA 95688
(707) 448-9454

St. Thomas Diving
5640 N. Blackstone
Fresno, CA 93710
(209) 449-8888

Stan's Skin Diving Shop
554 South Bascom Ave.
San Jose, CA 95128
(408) 294-7717

Stockton Aquatic Center
1127 W. Fremont St.
Stockton, CA 95203
(209) 467-3483

Subsurface Progression
18600 S. Hwy. 1
Fort Bragg, CA 95437
(707) 964-3793

Tri Valley Scuba
21310 San Ramon Valley Blvd.
San Ramon, CA 94583
(415) 828-5040

Ukiah Skin & Scuba
1900 No. State Street, #A
Ukiah, CA 95482
(707) 462-5396

Undersea Adventures
2830 Crow Canyon Road
San Ramon, CA 94583
(415) 838-2348

Vacaville Marine & Dive
170 Butcher Rd.
Vacaville, CA 95687
(707) 446-1025

Valley Scuba
347 Nord Ave., #3
Chico, CA 95926
(916) 891-5041

Wallin's Dive Store
517 E. Bayshore Road
Redwood City, CA 94063
(415) 369-2131

Wet Pleasure
2245 El Camino Real
Santa Clara, CA 95050
(408) 984-5819

DIVE TOUR OPERATOR

Landfall Productions
Destination Monterey
Dive Packages
6205 C Joaquin Murieta
Newark, CA 94560
1 (800) 525-3833 Out of California

1 (408) 246-4710 In California
Special dive packages for out-of-state divers

Index

Bold numbers indicate pages with photos.